READY, SET, DRAW!

EXTINCT AND ENDANGERED ANIMALS YOU CAN DRAW

Nicole Brecke

Patricia M. Stockland

Millbrook Press / Minneapolis

Edited by Mari Kesselring

Millbrook Press
A division of Lerner Publishing Group, Inc.
241 First Avenue North
Minneapolis, MN 55401 U.S.A.

Website address: www.lernerbooks.com

Library of Congress Cataloging-in-Publication Data

Brecke, Nicole.
    Extinct and endangered animals you can draw / by Nicole Brecke and Patricia M. Stockland ; illustrations by Nicole Brecke.
        p.   cm. — (Ready, set, draw!)
    Includes index.
    ISBN: 978–0–7613–4165–9 (lib. bdg. : alk. paper)
    1. Extinct animals in art—Juvenile literature. 2. Endangered species in art—Juvenile literature.
3. Drawing—Technique—Juvenile literature. I. Stockland, Patricia M. II. Title.
NC780.5.B74 2010
743.6—dc22   2009018141

Manufactured in the United States of America
1 – BP – 12/15/09

TABLE OF CONTENTS

ABOUT THIS BOOK

Gorillas, dodos, and rhinos! Round up a herd of exotic animals. With the help of this book, you can begin drawing these extinct and endangered creatures. Sketch a panda. Or draw a quagga. Soon you'll know how to create many amazing animals.

Follow these steps to create each animal. Each drawing begins with a basic form. The form is made up of a line and a couple of shapes. These lines and shapes will help you make your drawing the correct size.

A First, read all the steps and look at the pictures. Then use a pencil to lightly draw the line and shapes shown in RED. You will erase these lines later.

B Next, draw the lines shown in BLUE.

C Keep going! Once you have completed a step, the color of the line changes to BLACK. Follow the BLUE line until you're done.

WHAT YOU WILL NEED

PENCIL SHARPENER

COLORED PENCILS

HELPFUL HINTS

Be creative. Use your imagination. Read about pandas, saber-toothed cats, and woolly mammoths. Then follow the steps to sketch your own book of exciting animals.

Practice drawing different lines and shapes. All your drawings will start with these.

Use very light pencil lines when you are drawing.

ERASER

Helpful tips and hints will offer you good ideas on making the most of your sketch.

PENCIL

Colors are exciting. Try to use a variety of shades. This will add value, or depth, to your finished drawings.

PAPER

Keep practicing, and have fun!

HOW TO DRAW A QUAGGA

The quagga was a yellowish brown member of the zebra family. Quaggas only became extinct, or died out completely, in the late 1800s. This curious creature was native to southern African plains. People in those areas hunted quaggas for meat and leather. The species died out because of too much hunting. The quagga's spiky mane and striped head and neck made it quite a sight. Because of this, many quaggas were captured and sent to zoos around the world. Re-create your own colorful quagga in your drawing!

1 Draw a base circle and an angled baseline. Add two slightly larger base circles. Make the back by connecting the base circles.

2 Draw the ear, muzzle, and jaw. Use vertical lines for the legs. Add hooves. Draw a curved belly.

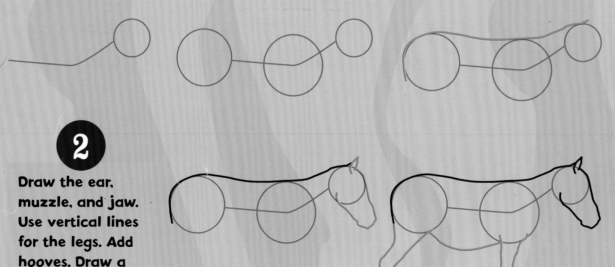

3

Add two
more legs
and hooves
and a neck.
Draw a spiky
mane and
thin tail.

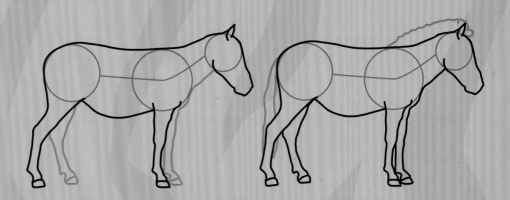

4 Carefully erase your baselines and shapes. Draw an eye, nostril,
and muzzle marking.

5 Now it's time to
color your quagga!

HOW TO DRAW A PANAMANIAN GOLDEN FROG

You'll find the Panamanian golden frog in zoos, but it's likely extinct in the wild. This little yellow frog is the national symbol of Panama. People there have long believed the golden frog brings good luck. In fact, when a Panamanian golden frog dies, legend says the animal turns into gold. Although that story is a myth, these small frogs do manage some amazing things. Panamanian golden frogs can't hear, so they wave to one another to communicate. Draw your own golden frog for good luck.

1

Lightly draw a long base oval and curved center line. Add a bumpy line down each side.

2

Draw the front leg and toes. Add the other front toes.

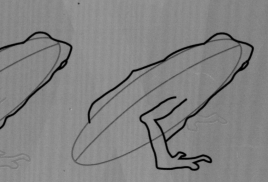

3

Draw the back leg and toes. Make a U shape for the hip. Add a curved line for the belly. Add a small bump.

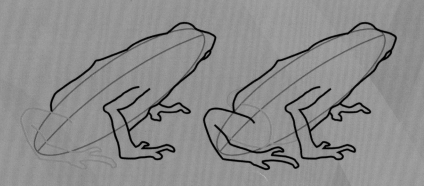

4 Carefully erase your center line and base shape. Add a large eye and two lines. Draw a pupil in the eye.

5 Now it's time to color your Panamanian golden frog!

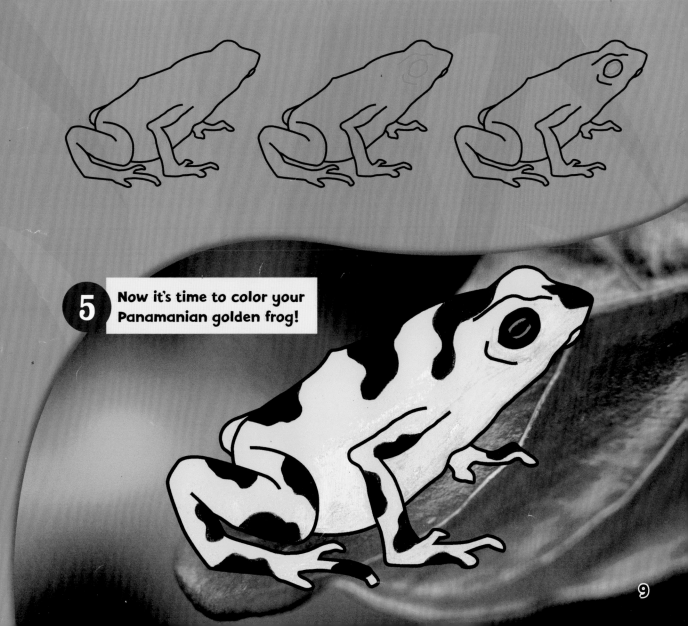

HOW TO DRAW A BLACK RHINOCEROS

The black rhinoceros is a symbol of power and strength. It can't see very well, but the rhino has a strong sense of hearing and smell. When a rhino decides to charge, watch out! This creature can weigh as much as a car. It can run at speeds of 30 miles (48 kilometers) per hour. But the rhino is also endangered. Poachers, or people who hunt illegally, have killed many rhinos throughout Africa. Hunting and a loss of habitat (the natural place in which an animal lives) have left rhinos in danger of becoming extinct.

1 Draw a light, small base oval and a curved center line. Add a larger base oval.

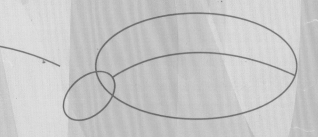

2 Add two horns, a pointed lip, and a curved jaw for the head. Draw a humped back and a long, skinny tail.

3 Use vertical lines to make the legs. Add a neck and curved belly. Draw the other two legs.

4 Carefully erase your base shapes and center line. Add a small nostril and small eye. Draw two ears.

5 Now it's time to color your black rhinoceros!

HOW TO DRAW A SABER-TOOTHED CAT

The saber-toothed cat was a giant ten thousand years ago. Its fierce teeth could grow up to 7 inches (18 centimeters) long! Now extinct, saber-toothed cats, or *Smilodons*, behaved much like modern lions. They lived in packs and hunted as a group, pouncing on prey rather than chasing it. Some people refer to the *Smilodon* as a "saber-toothed tiger," but this big creature was quite a bit different from the tigers we know today. The *Smilodon* had a bobbed tail and weighed about twice as much as a tiger.

1 Draw a base circle and a straight center line. Add two larger base circles.

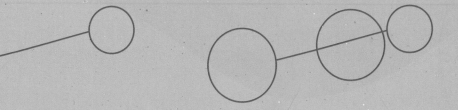

2 Draw the spine and tail by connecting the circle tops. Make a short back leg, paw, and belly.

3 Add the neck and a large front leg and paw. Use slight bumps and short lines to show muscles. Add the back leg and paw and the other front leg and paw.

4 Make the face and top of the muzzle. Add two small, pointy ears. Draw a large, long canine tooth and the bottom jaw.

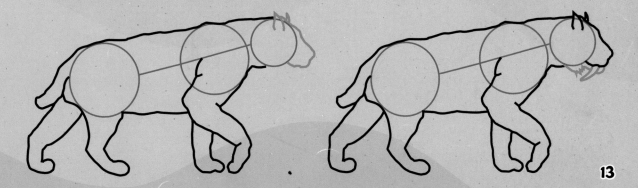

5

Carefully erase your baseline and shapes.

6

Add an eye and a nose.

MAKE TRACKS

Scientists have found fossilized paw prints of extinct creatures such as *Smilodon*.

DRAW A PAW PRINT!

A

B

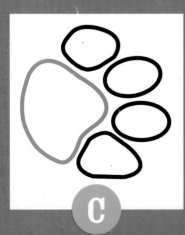

C

Smilodon fossils have been found in California.

7 Now it's time to color your saber-toothed cat!

5 Before finishing the face, carefully erase your base shapes and baseline.

6

Draw a heart shape for the nose area. Add a small mouth line underneath. Make an eye area above the nose shape. Add two small eyes and two nostrils. Draw two curved lines on the forehead.

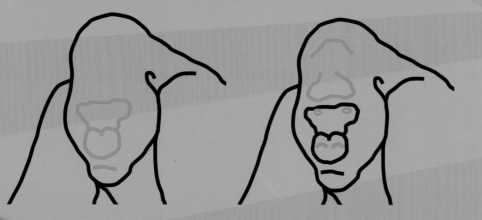

Did you know...
KOKO, A GORILLA BORN IN 1971, CAN USE SIGN LANGUAGE. SHE HAS LEARNED ABOUT 2,000 ENGLISH WORDS!

No two gorillas' nose prints are the same.

7 Now it's time to color your mountain gorilla!

HOW TO DRAW A
DODO BIRD

The dodo bird was once native to Mauritius, an African island east of Madagascar. Sailors began visiting the island in the 1500s. During the 1600s, the settlers brought animals such as monkeys and dogs to Mauritius. Between being hunted for human food and attacked by the new animals, the dodo became extinct before 1700. The dodo could sometimes protect itself with its very long, sharp, bent beak. But with a clumsy waddle, the dodo bird could not move around very quickly. It also had very short wings and was unable to fly.

1 Draw a small base circle and baseline. Add a larger base oval. Draw the top of the head, neck, and back.

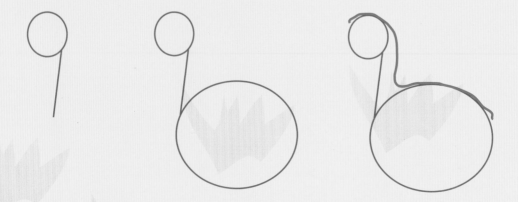

2 Make a long, bent beak and a short line. Add the bottom of the beak and a mouth line. Draw the front of the neck and chest.

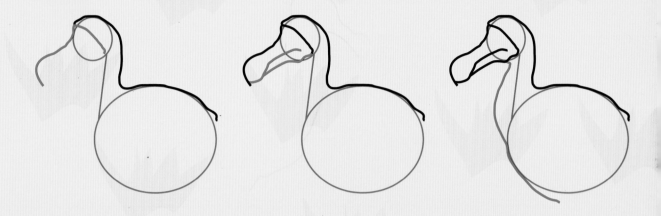

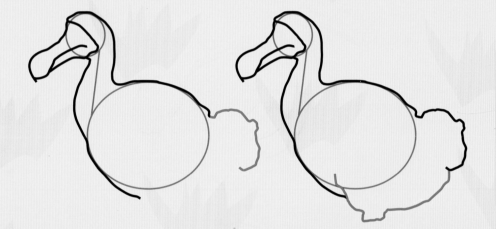

3 Draw a puffy tail. Add a larger half circle with a small bump to connect the tail and chest.

4 From the small bump, add a leg and talons. Draw the other leg and talons.

5 Draw a small wing. Add a line near the tail. Carefully erase your baselines.

6

Make a small eye. Add feather lines to the wing.

HATCH AN EGG

Scientists believe the dodo usually laid and hatched one egg at a time.

DRAW AN EGG AND A NEST!

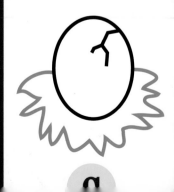

A   B   C

TRY THIS
Use shades of brown and gray to color your dodo bird's feathers.

7 Now it's time to color your dodo bird!

TO HELP DIGEST ITS FOOD, the dodo bird would eat large pebbles and even chunks of iron.

HOW TO DRAW A WOOLLY MAMMOTH

Just over ten thousand years ago, the woolly mammoth became extinct. Until then, this elephant-sized animal roamed North America as well as parts of Europe and Asia. You might recognize its large, long tusks. Some woolly mammoth tusks were 10 feet (3 meters) long. These tusks were some of the first fossil parts discovered by scientists. The woolly mammoth is a close ancestor, or relative, to the modern elephant. But the mammoth had bigger tusks—and a bigger appetite. It was also covered with lots of coarse hair and wool.

1

Lightly draw a base circle. Add a base oval near the top. Draw two baselines at the bottom.

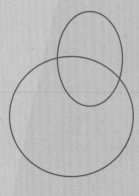
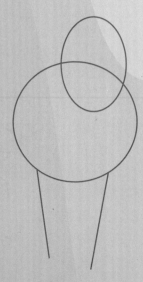

2

Draw two curving ears and the top of the head. Add two curved face lines inside the ear lines.

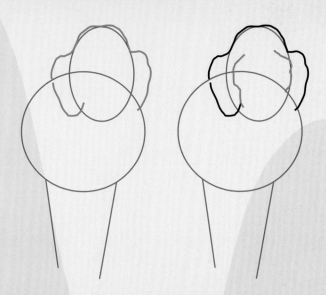

3 Use bumpy vertical lines to draw a long trunk. Add a dented oval to the end of the trunk. Draw a large, curved tusk and a shorter curved face line. Repeat this on the other side.

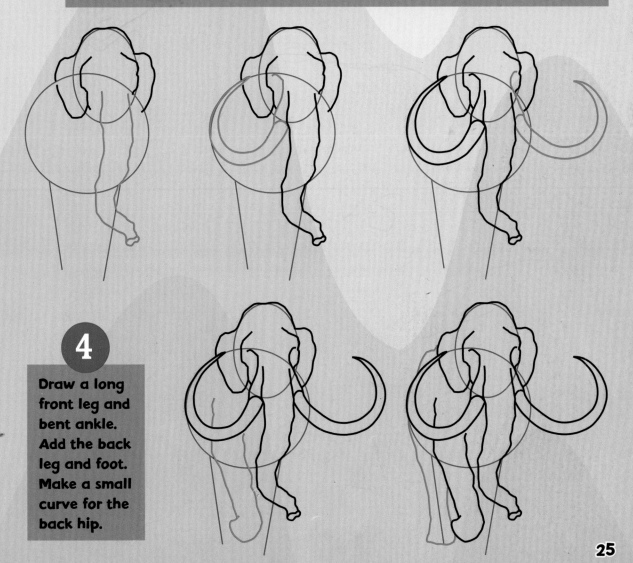

4

Draw a long front leg and bent ankle. Add the back leg and foot. Make a small curve for the back hip.

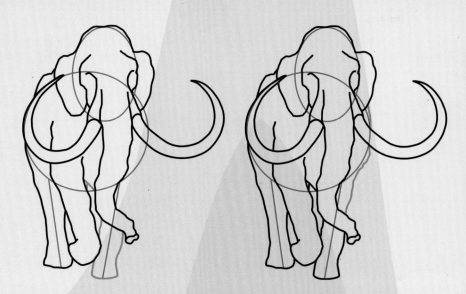

Draw the other front leg and foot. Make two very short lines between the trunk and first leg. Add a curving vertical line to finish the side.

6

Carefully erase your base shapes and lines.

7

Add two oval-shaped eyes.

No one knows exactly what caused the woolly mammoth's extinction.

8

Now it's time to color your woolly mammoth!

TRY THIS
Color with long strokes to show hair.

HOW TO DRAW A
GIANT PANDA

The giant panda is a familiar face among threatened species. It is the symbol for the World Wildlife Fund, or **WWF**. It is also endangered. Very few giant pandas remain in the wild. This shy black-and-white bear lives in the mountains of China. Although the giant panda is a bear, it does not eat meat. Pandas eat a diet almost entirely of bamboo. Because a panda needs to eat so much bamboo, it doesn't hibernate during the winter as other bears do. Instead, it spends winter and spring looking for more food.

1 Lightly draw a base circle and curved baseline. Add a base oval. Draw a round head inside the circle. Add two ears on top of the head.

2 Make a rough L shape around the oval. Add a short leg. Draw a small bent line from the face. Use a curving line to finish the front leg and paw.

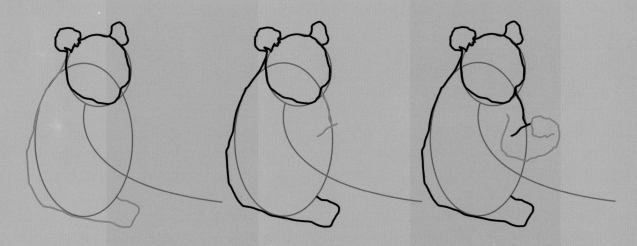

3 Draw a long, bent, bumpy V shape for the other front leg and paw. Add two short lines to the back leg. Draw the other back leg.

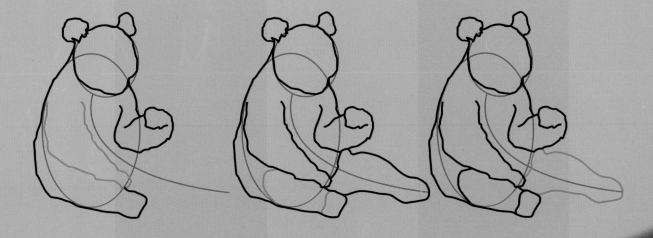

Fast Fact...

THE GIANT PANDA IS VERY GOOD AT CLIMBING TREES.

4 Carefully erase your baseline and shapes. Add short lines for markings.

5 Draw a nose and a small mouth. Add curved ovals for eye markings. Make longer lines down from each to finish the muzzle. Add two small eyes.

FEED ME

Pandas need to eat a lot of bamboo to stay healthy.

DRAW A BAMBOO STALK!

A

B

C

TRY THIS
Erase the bamboo stalk where the panda's paw overlaps.

6 Now it's time to color your giant panda!

31

FURTHER READING

Burnie, David, and Tony Juniper. *Endangered Planet*. Boston: Kingfisher, 2004.

Goodman, Susan E. *Saber-Toothed Cats*. Minneapolis: Millbrook Press, 2006.

Gunzi, Christiane. *The Best Book of Endangered and Extinct Animals*. Boston: Kingfisher, 2004.

Kids' Planet
http://www.kidsplanet.org

U.S. Fish & Wildlife Service: Kids' Corner
http://www.fws.gov/endangered/kids

Walker, Sally M. *Rhinos*. Rev. ed. Minneapolis: Lerner Publications Company, 2007.

World Wildlife Fund
http://www.worldwildlife.org

INDEX